Saving Tomato Day

Story by Rose Inserra
Illustrations by Fuuji Takashi

Saving Tomato Day

Text: Rose Inserra
Publishers: Tania Mazzeo and Eliza Webb
Series consultant: Amanda Sutera
  Hands on Heads Consulting
Editor: Kirsty Hine
Project editor: Annabel Smith
Designer: Jess Kelly
Project designer: Danielle Maccarone
Illustrations: Fuuji Takashi
Production controller: Renee Tome

NovaStar

Text © 2024 Cengage Learning Australia Pty Limited
Illustrations © 2024 Cengage Learning Australia Pty Limited

Copyright Notice
This Work is copyright. No part of this Work may be reproduced, stored in a retrieval system, or transmitted in any form or by any means without prior written permission of the Publisher. Except as permitted under the *Copyright Act 1968*, for example any fair dealing for the purposes of private study, research, criticism or review, subject to certain limitations. These limitations include: Restricting the copying to a maximum of one chapter or 10% of this book, whichever is greater; Providing an appropriate notice and warning with the copies of the Work disseminated; Taking all reasonable steps to limit access to these copies to people authorised to receive these copies; Ensuring you hold the appropriate Licences issued by the Copyright Agency Limited ("CAL"), supply a remuneration notice to CAL and pay any required fees.

ISBN 978 0 17 033434 1

Cengage Learning Australia
Level 5, 80 Dorcas Street
Southbank VIC 3006 Australia
Phone: 1300 790 853
Email: aust.nelsonprimary@cengage.com

For learning solutions, visit **cengage.com.au**

Printed in China by 1010 Printing International Ltd
1 2 3 4 5 6 7 28 27 26 25 24

Nelson acknowledges the Traditional Owners and Custodians of the lands of all First Nations Peoples. We pay respect to Elders past and present, and extend that respect to all First Nations Peoples today.

Contents

Italian Words in This Book

Here is a list of Italian words that appear in this book and what they mean.

biscotti (*bis-ko-tee*) – biscuits

bravo (*brah-vo*) – well done

ciao (*chow*) – hi; bye

grazie (*graht-siyeh*) – thank you

mamma mia (*muh-mah-mee-ah*) – oh my goodness

mangia (*mahn-jah*) – eat

nonna (*noh-nah*) – grandma

nonno (*noh-noh*) – grandpa

passata (*puh-sah-tah*) – tomato pasta sauce

zia (*zee-ah*) – aunt

zio (*zee-oh*) – uncle

Chapter 1

No Tomatoes

"Oh, no!" Mum cried out on the phone to Dad. "What do you mean there are no tomatoes left?"

Dad was on speaker. "The fruit and vegetable shop lost our order," he said, sounding upset. "I've driven to so many places this morning but there are no Roma tomatoes left."

Mum looked downcast as she ended the call.

"Can we use any other kind of tomatoes?" I asked.

Mum shook her head. "They have to be Roma tomatoes. They're perfect for making passata. They're juicy and small. And we need at least five boxes."

"We'll find some," I said, hoping for some luck.

"Mamma mia!" cried Mum. "How do we tell Nonna? It's Tomato Day tomorrow!"

For those of you who don't know, my family is Italian and Tomato Day is a very special day for us. It happens once a year, on a Sunday, in the middle of summer when tomatoes are ripe and juicy.

We get together with the whole family – my zia, zio, cousins and anyone else who can make it – at Nonna's house to make passata. Passata is what we use for our pasta sauce, and we make enough passata to last the family for the entire year.

Nonna is always especially excited about Tomato Day. It's an old family tradition that she has been part of since she was a little girl living in a small town in Italy.

Some of my favourite memories as a little kid are from Tomato Day.

"Marco, what are we going to do?"
Mum said to me. Her voice was filled with
sadness. "We can't wait another week to
make passata. Nonna is moving house next
weekend, and this is the last Sunday we'll
have together in that house."

Nonna's house was too big for her now, without Nonno. It was the house that she and Nonno had bought together after they got married, and where my dad and Zio Joe grew up. But now she was moving to a smaller place. And that's why she wanted one last Tomato Day in the house that was filled with so many happy memories.

When Dad came home, he looked exhausted. "I've driven all over and I can't find any Roma tomatoes."

"Nonna is going to be so disappointed," I said.

In case you're wondering why Tomato Day is so important to us, it's because the day is about more than just making passata – it's about spending time with the whole family. It makes Nonna happy to have her family together so that the tradition can be passed down to the younger family members. I help Nonna make passata every year, and I learn more each time we make it.

Just then, I had an idea. "My friend Ali could help!" I said. "His family has that fruit and vegetable stand at the local market. I'm sure we could find some Roma tomatoes there!"

Mum and Dad's faces suddenly lit up, their eyes filling with hope.

"I had forgotten all about that. Thanks for the reminder, Marco!" said Dad.

"Great idea. Let's go!" said Mum.

I ran to the front door, feeling excited at last.

Chapter 2

At the Market

The market was bustling with people. It was noisy and filled with all sorts of smells – spices, fish, doughnuts and delicious hot foods. Mum, Dad and I hurried along.

I finally found Ali at his family's fruit and vegetable stand. I rushed over to him. He looked surprised to see me. "Marco, what are you doing here?" he asked.

"We're looking for Roma tomatoes to make passata," I replied, a little out of breath. "Do you have any here?"

"I'll ask Dad," replied Ali. "Just a minute."

I crossed my fingers and waited anxiously. Mum and Dad looked worried.

A few minutes later, Ali's dad had bad news. "Sorry, we don't have any left. We sold every single box of Roma tomatoes earlier today," he said.

He offered to ask some of the other market stallholders.

"Don't worry, Marco," said Ali. "My dad and I will help you find the tomatoes."

Mum and Ali's dad exchanged phone numbers. Mum texted Nonna's house address to Ali's dad. If he and Ali did find some tomatoes, they would know where to deliver them.

I know you don't know my Nonna the way I do, but you have no idea how much it would mean to her to have one last Tomato Day at her house before she moved. Nonna would be overjoyed. I could almost hear her shouting, "Bravo! Bravo!"

But for now, we had to break the bad news to her. We left the market and drove to Nonna's house.

Chapter 3

Breaking the News

Nonna was outside before we even got to the front door.

"Ciao. Come in. I've just baked some biscotti," said Nonna. She gave me a big hug and kiss on the cheek.

My mouth watered. I could almost taste Nonna's delicious Italian biscuits. Nonna is an amazing cook. Making and sharing food is one of the ways that she shows love.

Nonna looked over my shoulder. "Where are the tomatoes?"

"We couldn't find any ..." Dad began to say.

"But my friend Ali and his dad are looking for some," I interrupted, trying not to disappoint Nonna.

"Mamma mia!" Nonna cried, holding her hand to her mouth. "This is terrible! And I just found out that your cousins have chicken pox and can't come tomorrow. Your Zio Joe and Zia Grace have to look after them, so they won't be here either. I really wanted the whole family here together one last time."

Nonna's eyes watered. I was sad, too. I loved being with my cousins Bella and Sofia on Tomato Day.

We sat down to have Nonna's biscotti. I had hot chocolate and Mum and Dad had coffee. "These bottles," Nonna said, pointing to the bottles behind us, "have been re-used every year for over twenty years!"

Nonna then told us the story, as she had many times before, of when she was seven years old and came here from Italy with her family. She said that she helped make passata with her parents because there was no passata in shops back then. Other Italian friends and family who had migrated helped, too. Her family grew their own tomatoes. Others bought the tomatoes from farmers. Everyone grew basil in their gardens and picked it fresh on Tomato Day, adding it to the bottles of passata.

We waited for hours for Ali's dad to message with news. Just as we had almost given up hope, a white van pulled up outside Nonna's house. It was Ali and his dad! We rushed outside to greet them.

"Hi," said Ali. "We have a box of Roma tomatoes for you!"

"Thank you," said Nonna in a small voice. "But we need five boxes."

"Maybe we should cancel Tomato Day this year," Mum said.

Nonna looked miserable. She had prepared everything for tomorrow. All the bottles for the passata had been washed. The electric tomato-juicing machine and bottle-top machine to attach the lids were checked and cleaned. And the basil was ready to be picked from Nonna's garden.

"Don't worry, we'll find more," said Ali.

"Don't give up hope, Nonna," I told her.

Chapter 4

A Special Delivery

The next morning, Mum, Dad and I arrived at Nonna's house at seven o'clock. Nonna's favourite music was playing in the garage. She always played music on Tomato Day.

Nonna looked tired. I offered to get her some coffee and then we all sat down at the kitchen table. Suddenly, there was the sound of a car horn tooting. It was Ali's dad's van! We ran outside just as Ali was opening the back door of the van – four large boxes of Roma tomatoes were stacked in a pile!

"You found more tomatoes!" Nonna exclaimed. "Grazie! Grazie!" she said, and hugged Ali and his dad.

"Yes," said Ali. "We found them at a farm nearby. They were the farmer's last four boxes of Roma tomatoes."

Thanks to Ali and his dad, Tomato Day had been saved!

Ali and his dad decided to stay to help make the passata. His mum and younger sister, Sami, came over too. We were ready to get to work.

I showed Ali and Sami how to load small buckets with tomatoes and wash them. Then, after the adults cut up the tomatoes and put them through the juicing machine, I poured the passata into the bottles. Sami dropped a basil leaf in the bottle before Ali sealed the bottle with a lid.

"It's ten o'clock and we've finished two boxes already," said Nonna. "Good job, everyone!"

And then, everything stopped. The lights in the garage went out. The music went silent. The tomato-juicing machine stopped working.

The power had gone out!

Nonna's phone beeped at that moment. It was a message from the power company. The power was going to be out for the rest of the day in her street!

We would have to finish making the passata without power.

The power is out on your street until 9 pm today.

Chapter 5

People Power

"Don't worry everyone," said Nonna. "I have an old tomato-juicing machine with a handle somewhere. It doesn't need power."

"I'll help you find it," I called out.

After looking through some old boxes, I found the old machine. Nonna gave it a good clean and in a few minutes she had set it up. We could keep working!

We found some solar fairy lights and draped them around the garage. Nonna even found an old battery-powered radio. It felt like a party – except we had to work!

The old machine was very slow and our arms got sore turning the handle, but we kept going.

It was soon lunchtime. Dad fired up the pizza oven and prepared some pizzas.

"Mangia! Mangia!" said Nonna, when the pizzas were ready. "It will help you to keep working!"

"We'll need more people to help us finish the passata," said Mum, looking a little tired. "Everyone's arms are getting sore using the old machine."

At that moment, Mr Singh from next door walked into the garage. The smell of pizza and the sound of music had attracted him to Nonna's garage. His face lit up when he saw us all working together. "This is wonderful!" he said.

That's when I had a brilliant idea. I always think better after a slice of pizza fresh from Nonna's pizza oven.

"Nonna, we can use your neighbourhood's group chat on your phone to let everyone know we need help. I'm sure some of the neighbours will have more fun here than sitting at home with no power!" I said.

"Bravo! You're a genius!" Nonna said, and gave me her phone after she gave me another big kiss on the cheek.

"Well, genius," laughed Ali, "I think you should take a photo of the pizzas and the fairy lights and post it on the group chat. Everyone loves a pizza party!"

In minutes, Nonna's garage was buzzing with people – young and old. All neighbours, all happy to help – and eat pizza, too!

Before long, we had finished making all the passata. I took more photos and posted them on the group chat site, adding a comment:

Same time next year! New place – my house. Free bottle of passata and pizza for all helpers!

Ali smiled. "Great idea," he said. "We're definitely coming to your house next year."

Nonna came over and gave me a big hug. "Thank you, Marco. You made this Tomato Day very special for me. I can't wait for the tradition to continue next year at your house."

"Sure, Nonna. And we know just where to get the tomatoes from, right?" I said, and winked at Ali.